The Government's Draft Legislative Programme – Summary of consultation

Presented to Parliament
By the Lord Privy Seal, Leader of the House of Commons
and Minister for Women and Equality
December 2008

Cm 7561 £19.15

ISBN: 978 0 10 175612 9

Contents

Foreword – Leader of the House of Commons

The Rt Hon Harriet Harman QC MP
Leader of the House of Commons

The Government has for the second year published its Draft Legislative Programme, in advance of the Queen's Speech on 3 December. On publication in May we promised to produce a summary of consultation responses.

This document sets out the wide ranging responses received. Building on the experience of the first consultation last year we began the process two months earlier and the longer time allowed for a wider involvement by the public.

We are determined to seek greater engagement not just with Parliament but also with the public. This consultation process is an important step in that direction. Regional events across the country, including a national day of Consultation on 11 July in which myself and other Cabinet Ministers took part, were useful in enabling face to face debate.

The Government also built on last year's consultation with new methods including an online questionnaire on the Leader of the Commons' website, and the chance to respond by post through a freepost address, as well as online opportunities to comment on individual Bills.

Consulting the public should be a continuous process for Government and finding new ways of engagement will help make for better laws. The Government's priorities for economic stability and helping people make the most of their potential were key themes within the Draft Legislative Programme.

The summary demonstrates the Government's commitment to greater transparency and openness to the public in the legislative process and also points the way forward for helping people to get more involved in holding the Government to account not just during elections but in the day to day work of Parliament and the Government. We aim to build the confidence of the public in understanding how the political process makes a difference to everyday lives and this consultation process is a useful step in that direction.

HARRIET HARMAN

Executive Summary of the Draft Legislative Programme consultation

1. This is the second year in which the Government has published its *Draft Legislative Programme*. In *Preparing Britain for the Future: The Government's Draft Legislative Programme 2008/09*, published on 14 May 2008, the Government committed to publish a summary of consultation responses. The consultation period closed on 6 August 2008 and comments were received from people across the United Kingdom. This document comprises that summary and a response in the form of the changes that have been made to the programme that was announced by Her Majesty the Queen in her Speech to Parliament on 3 December 2008.

2. This year, the consultation process began two months earlier than last year to allow more time for comments. The consultation process has provided a means by which public comments can be fed into the legislative programme which has been finalised, taking into account these comments and the Government's priorities, in the Queen's Speech. It has also increased the transparency of the legislative process and raised the public's awareness of it.

3. The consultation process consisted of:

   - Regional events, mostly hosted by regional ministers and including a National Day of Consultation (11 July) when events took place across the country;
   - The Secretaries of State for Scotland, Wales and Northern Ireland wrote to a range of stakeholders encouraging them to take part in the consultation;
   - Short parliamentary debates took place in both Houses following the Prime Minister's statement on 14 May (repeated in the Lords on the same day) and a specific debate led by the Leader of the House of Commons in that House on 26 June;
   - A questionnaire on the Leader's website (www.commonsleader.gov.uk) and the territorial offices about the Draft Legislative Programme for members of the public to complete;
   - An opportunity to make online comments on individual Bills and suggestions for different Bills to be created;

- Responses by post, both to a freepost address set up for the purpose, and directly to the Leader of the House and the territorial offices;
- Distributing 30,000 'Making Your Voice Heard' leaflets to public libraries with response sections; and
- A review of responses by the e-Politix website.

4. The consultation received the views of around 2,000 people and organisations, comprising 751 responses to the Leader's website, around 1,200 people and organisations who participated in the 58 regional events and 44 individuals and 58 organisations who responded by post. The total cost of the consultation was £30,922.38 including the cost of regional events, leaflets and website.

5. In addition to comments received through this consultation, many departments ran their own detailed consultation on the proposals in the bills. It is therefore important to read this document alongside the other consultation responses. For example the NHS Reform Bill proposals were necessarily high-level so as not to pre-empt Lord Darzi's report *High Quality Care for All*. This was published in June 2008, following an extensive consultation exercise. A consultation was launched alongside the report seeking views on the proposed NHS Constitution, referred to in the Draft Legislative Programme.

6. Typically each Bill received between about 5 and 100 comments on the Leader's website, although Bills attracted additional specific comments throughout the consultation process. Bills which drew particular interest (at least 50 comments throughout the consultation) included:
   - The Equality Bill attracted both positive and negative comments particularly from the lesbian, gay, bisexual groups and transgender community;
   - Positive comments on the NHS Reform Bill and the Policing and Crime Reduction Bill were received, although a number of respondents called for the inclusion of legislation relating to unpaid carers within the former;
   - The Communications Data Bill attracted some criticism from people who were concerned about data protection issues and the development of a 'nanny state'. The Saving Gateway Bill also attracted some criticism from those who felt that benefits were generous enough.

6. Many people were uncertain about how the legislative process worked, so the Government received a limited number of specific comments. Many people preferred to comment on the themes of the programme, which most people agreed were the right ones in principle. These were:

    - Economic stability
    - Making the most of your potential
    - Personalisation and Improvement of Public Services
    - Handing back power to the people

7. Most people commented on individual issues relevant to them which were not in the programme, for example calls for a referendum on EU membership and the Lisbon Treaty, about the funding arrangements for the devolved administrations and to reduce immigration. As a result of the comments made it is therefore hard to draw specific conclusions about peoples' views on the content of the programme.

8. Members of the public and organisations appreciated being consulted on the Draft Legislative Programme. However, there was some distrust of the value of the consultation process. Some people felt that their views were unlikely to lead to any real change. This summary response sets out where the programme as presented in the Queen's Speech has changed from the Draft Legislative Programme.

9. The Government believes that the results of this consultation have a wider benefit beyond taking into account people's views on the specific detail of the programme, as it demonstrates the Government's ongoing commitment to greater transparency and openness to the public in the legislative process.

ONE – List of Bills in the Draft Legislative Programme

The following bills were included in the DLP:

Economic stability

1. Banking Reform Bill
2. Saving Gateway Bill
3. Business Rate Supplements Bill
4. Marine and Coastal Access Bill
5. Heritage Protection Bill

Making the most of your potential

6. Education and Skills Bill
7. Equality Bill
8. Welfare Reform Bill

Personalisation and improvement of public services

9. Policing and Crime Reduction Bill
10. Transport Security Bill
11. Communications Data Bill
12. Law Reform, Victims and Witnesses Bill
13. Citizenship, Immigration and Borders Bill
14. Coroners and Death Certification Bill
15. National Health Service Reform Bill

Handing back power to the people

16. Constitutional Renewal Bill
17. Community Empowerment, Housing and Economic Regeneration Bill

Other

18. Geneva Conventions and United Nations Personnel Bill

The following Bills have subsequently been renamed:

- The National Health Service Reform Bill is now the Health Bill;
- The Community Empowerment, Housing and Economic Regeneration Bill is now the Local Democracy, Economic Development and Construction Bill;
- The Education and Skills Bill is now the Children, Skills and Learning Bill.

However, the Bills will be referred to by their original names throughout this document. Other more significant changes are detailed in the next chapter.

This document includes a summary of the comments made during the public consultation and, where relevant, a Government response to the points made. For ease of reading, these responses have been included in the body of the text in italics.

TWO – What has changed since the Draft Legislative Programme?

The key benefit of publishing the legislative programme in draft is to open up a previously closed process and to enable greater transparency. This allows both the public and parliamentarians to see the Government's legislative plans for the coming year as they are developing. It also gives more time to begin to consider and debate those plans, thus increasing their influence. The value of the consultation on this document is not just based on the number of responses received, but also on the raised awareness amongst the public of the legislative process.

Many respondents expressed a wish that the consultation would lead to meaningful change to the legislative programme. The overall messages that have come out of the consultation in relation to the Government's broad priorities, and the support for individual measures, have been taken into account and do influence thinking as the legislative programme is put together in future years. For example, there was general agreement in the consultation that the themes of the programme were the right ones for the Government to be concentrating on. Also consideration will be undertaken in Government departments on ideas for new bills, in planning their future bids for legislation.

Following the close of the consultation on 6 August, the summary of responses was considered by the Leader of the House of Commons who then put the summary before the Prime Minister and the Cabinet, at the same time as the Cabinet discussed and agreed the final content of the legislative programme.

The following changes have been made to the final programme:

- The Banking Bill has already been introduced to Parliament in October, ahead of the Queen's Speech, in view of the current economic climate and the urgent need to reform the banking system and strengthen depositor protection. The Government hopes that this will enable this legislation to complete its parliamentary passage and become law shortly;
- The Child Poverty Bill has been included in the programme to set in law the Prime Minister's commitment to eradicate child poverty by 2020;

- The Communications Data Bill will not form part of the programme. The Government has announced a public consultation in the New Year. Dependent on the outcome of this consultation, the Government may publish draft legislation later in the 2008-09 session;
- The Heritage Protection Bill will not form part of the programme although the Government remains committed to this legislation. It will be brought forward at a later date as soon as parliamentary time allows;
- The Transport Security Bill will not form part of the programme as a separate measure, but important provisions on airport security will be taken forward this year in the Policing and Crime Bill;
- Further consideration is being given to how we meet our international maritime security obligations including a review of what further legislation might be required in the light of recent events, including piracy;
- Further consideration is being given to how to take forward the provisions of the Geneva Conventions and United Nations Personnel Bill;
- The Coroners and Death Certification Bill will not form part of the programme as a separate measure, but its key provisions will be combined with the Law Reform, Victims and Witnesses Bill to be called the Coroners and Justice Bill. The Government's reforms of the justice and coroners systems are motivated by a common purpose, namely to deliver a more effective, transparent and responsive service to the public. It is also the case that there are often close links between the criminal justice system and coroners' investigations;
- The Borders, Immigration and Citizenship Bill will not include provisions for the simplification of immigration legislation. The Government is committed to the comprehensive reform of immigration law – a major undertaking which it is more important to do well than to do quickly. The Government will build on the pre-legislative scrutiny of the partial draft bill that was published in July and will publish all its provisions in draft for full consultation and will bring these provisions forward at a later date as soon as parliamentary time allows;

- Other provisions have been added to bills already in the programme, for example, action on Foreign Travel Orders for paedophiles, increased controls on binge and underage drinking, measures to increase local say on lap dancing clubs, simplifying and modernising the offence of assisting suicide and enabling the courts to pass an indeterminate sentence for public protection for certain terrorist offences;
- The Single Civil and Family Courts Bill will no longer be published in draft, following consultation with the Judiciary. However, in addition to the other draft bills mentioned in the Draft Legislative Programme, the Government will also be publishing further bills in draft relating to community empowerment and the protection of the environmental resources of Antarctica;
- Work is continuing on developing the proposals set out in the draft Constitutional Renewal Bill which was published in March 2008.

THREE – Events

In order to consult as wide a section of the public as possible, the Regional Ministers co-ordinated consultation events across the country. These events were given a focus by the National Day of Consultation, on 11 July, but other events took place over the consultation period, which formally ended on 6 August.

Regional Ministers were first appointed by the Prime Minister on 28 June 2007 in order to give regions a clear sense of strategic direction. The remit of these Ministers includes giving citizens a voice in central government, ensuring that government policy takes account of the differing needs of the nine English regions. Regional Ministers make central government more visible in the regions, helping to raise its profile and generate awareness of the political system. As a consequence, they played a key role in the public consultation on the Draft Legislative Programme.

The purpose of the regional engagement events was to engage with, listen to and record the views of people on the proposals in the Draft Legislative Programme. Many, but not all, of the events were attended by a Minister. Discussions of the Draft Legislation Programme were included in some existing events, as well as at stand-alone events. Regional events were held in schools, Council offices, over breakfasts and lunches, with members of the public and the press, and advertised by newspaper, the internet and word of mouth.

Summary of events

The following events took place around the United Kingdom:

Region	Event
North East	**10 April** – meeting with the Strategic Health Authority to discuss the Embryology Bill and forthcoming health Legislation (pre-DLP launch consultation). **18 April** – meeting with the Vice Chancellors of the five Universities based in the North East and the Open University to discuss legislation affecting the Learning and Skills Council and the Higher Education sector in the North East (pre-DLP launch consultation). **23 May** – providing the key note speech at a Government Office North East Stakeholder Event, which reflected on the success of last year's consultation events and encouraged further engagement this year. **27 May** – consultation with Civic Society. **28 May** – consultation with Business groups. **28 May** – consultation with regional Trades Union Council. **29 May** – consultation with Leaders of 12 Strategic Local Authorities. **6 June** – meeting with the Northern Business Forum. **11 July** – two public events held in Teeside and Tyneside, hosted by the Evening Chronicle and the Evening Gazette.
North West	**2 June** – meeting with Merseyside media. **11 June** – Interviews with four newspapers. **13 June** – programme of interviews with key regional media. **19 June** – consultation event at Stretford High School with young people, teachers, parents & governors. **23 June** – breakfast meeting with business groups. **27 June** – North West Community Safety Managers Forum discussion. **29 June** – debate at NW Youth Parliament. **14 July** – consultation event with equality and diversity groups & third sector representatives in Merseyside. **16 July** – Interview with Business Insider (regional business magazine). A video message promoting the consultation was available on Government Office for the North West's website throughout.

Region	Event
Yorkshire and the Humber	**22 May** – event with York University politics students. **23 May** – Black and Minority Ethnic Voluntary and Community Sector regional panel meeting. **17 June** – discussion at Rural Affairs Forum. **17 June** – meeting with Chief Executives and Regional Directors of Government Agencies, and local authority, city and regional leaders. **23 June** – discussion with Regional Empowerment Consortium with Regional Faith Forum. **23 June** – meeting with cultural agencies. **30 June** – discussion with sixth form students, Garforth Community College, York. **11 July** – Stakeholder conference in Leeds.
London	**23 June** – interactive event for young Londoners. **11 July** – facilitated discussion with front-line public service staff in Lambeth, including police officers, teachers and social workers, about the Government's plans for the improvement and personalisation of public services.
South West	**19 June** – Dorset Third Sector Conference. **23 June** – discussion with students in Torbay, South Devon College. **11 July** – event in Exeter with Regional Director.
East Midlands	**12 June** – Employment Skills Partnership event. **8 July** – meeting with 9 County Councillors. **15 July** – roundtable event with the East Midlands Business Forum. **28 July** – discussion with the East Midlands Rural Consultation Forum.
West Midlands	**16 June** – meeting with employers in Birmingham. **23 June** – interview with Business Editor of the Stoke on Trent Sentinel. **30 June** – speech at the One Year On event in Birmingham. **7 July** – taking part in the Science and Innovation event in Worcester. **10 July** – dinner and discussion with business organisations. **21 July** – taking part in the West Midlands Businesses Open Gateway event in Birmingham. **28 July** – discussion at a Black Country science day.

Region	Event
East of England	**23 May** – speech to training providers and Business Reps. **6 June** – discussion at a Regional Partnership Group Meeting. **9 June** – discussion with stakeholders on the Suffolk coast. **2 July** – speech at a growth conference in Cambridge. **11 July** – public discussion event.
South East	**19 May** – discussion at a South East District Leaders Meeting. **9 June** – discussion at a Stakeholder Advisory Group. **11 June** – participating in a skills event in Reading. **8 July** – engaging with key stakeholders including business at the South East Skills Summit. **11 July** – interactive consultation event with young students at Defra's Innovation Unit in Reading. **14 July** – open stakeholder meeting for third sector representatives and key regional stakeholders in London.
Wales	**22 May** – round table discussion at the TUC Conference in Llandudno. **20 May** – event with Public Affairs for Cymru. **9 June** – meeting with the Police Federation for Wales. **11 July** – round table discussion with Bridgend College students. **11 July** – event in Cardiff with businesses from Wales.
Northern Ireland	**21 July** – meeting with stakeholders.

1. How was the Draft Legislative Programme received by the stakeholders?

Many members of the public from a variety of regions across the United Kingdom welcomed the chance to comment on the Draft Legislative Programme. It was clear from the responses to the consultation events that this development in the legislative process was a positive one, and was appreciated by the majority of those who attended. Members of the public felt particularly positive about the attendance of Ministers at many of the consultation events. They were pleased that their views were being listened to directly by Members of Parliament, and therefore felt more confident that account would be taken of their views.

Many people who attended the regional events were more interested in local, specific issues, than in the particular draft bills that were contained in the Draft Legislative Programme. Others were keen to discuss issues such as crime, education and health, but not specifically in the context of the proposals in the Bills. Very few people had read, or had knowledge of the detail, of the Draft Legislative Programme. When people commented on broader issues in their own terms, they often tended to attach these to the draft bill with the most relevant short title. In other cases, people connected with the themes of the Programme as opposed to its detail.

In Wales, members of the public at one event felt that the Draft Legislative Programme was not written plainly enough, and suggested that a version aimed specifically at youth readers should be published.

In Northern Ireland, while it was felt that there should be common themes in Northern Ireland and the rest of the UK, dealing with parallel policy agendas that might in the future diverge was recognised as a challenge.

2. Which Bills were discussed in detail?

Most regional consultations discussed a wide range of bills by name, but as described above, the names of the Bills were often used as a way for members of the public to raise specific, local issues, or to make general and wide-ranging points that did not relate specifically to the named bills.

In these regional discussions, the Bills that were raised the most often were:

- Policing and Crime Reduction Bill
- Education and Skills Bill
- Welfare Reform Bill
- Saving Gateway Bill

- Community Empowerment, Housing and Economic Regeneration Bill

Additionally, all four of the themes of the Draft Legislative Programme were raised equally frequently.

Those Bills that were raised the least frequently were:

- Coroners and Death Certification Bill
- Geneva Conventions and United Nations Personnel Bill
- Constitutional Renewal Bill
- Communications Data Bill

This division between more and less popular bills correlates with the observation that members of the public were more interested in discussing issues that did not relate to the detail of legislation, but that were broadly related to key issues like crime and education that affect their daily lives.

3. How do you think the event was received overall?

Almost all events were received very well by the public. People welcomed the chance to give feedback on the workings of Government, and at many events the attendees were vocal in their support for the proceedings.

Some respondents in the North East felt confident that this type of consultation would improve legislation, while those in a number of other regions felt the opposite, that the consultation was not likely to have a significant effect on the process of making legislation. In order to demonstrate that the consultation was having a real effect on legislation, respondents in the North East in particular asked for evidence that their comments were being fed into the decision-making process, and that change was resulting from this. These same respondents wanted to know why they had not been listened to before in this process, and were suspicious about the motives of the Government in producing the Draft Legislative Programme now. They also pointed out that there had not been a public consultation on other important issues such as the war in Iraq. Many young people in the North West who participated in the consultation events felt pleased that they were being consulted and said they valued having the opportunity to meet with Ministers and senior officials. They believed that the Government was serious about listening, and could point to changes in policy they feel they had influenced.

Many of the events were extremely well attended. The number of people involved in the consultation was increased further by the use of existing events as platforms on which to debate the Draft Legislative Programme.

4. Overall, would you say the themes, bills and other action outlined match your own priorities for what you think the Government should be doing?

Most of the people consulted on this issue felt that, in broad and general terms, the Draft Legislative Programme did match their own priorities on what the Government should be doing. In the detail, however, most respondents were able to name particular causes or issues that they felt the Government should be specifically tackling. People often failed to make a connection between the generalities of the bills and specific issues that they were keen to see pursued by the Government. When respondents did speak about general themes, they again focused on issues such as crime, education and health.

Government Response: *The bills that were outlined in the Draft Legislative Programme were, by necessity, described in general terms only. This is because the detail of the bills had either not been confirmed at the time of publishing the Draft Legislative Programme or was too detailed to merit inclusion. Each bill was described in one or two pages which outlined their purpose, main elements and main benefits, as well as consultations that had been taken on them, their territorial extent, and other actions that were taken in relation to them.*

Respondents in the East Midlands felt that access to the countryside was important and under-represented. Those in the South West focused on measures for young people and affordable housing, and called for a bill aimed specifically at small businesses. Those in the South East wanted to see more benefits for 15-17 year olds.

People in the North West and in Yorkshire and the Humber felt that the Government should be doing more to promote environmental priorities, while some respondents in the West Midlands felt that there were too many laws already, and therefore that legislative activity should be limited. Those in the North East were happy to see the four themes used in the Draft Legislative Programme, and felt that 'Making the Most of Your Potential' was particularly apposite in the current political climate. A number of commentators in London, the North West, and Yorkshire and the Humber wanted to see more being done to focus on development of positive activities and greater opportunities in work and training, particularly for the young.

5. Are the themes the right priorities for the Government to introduce new legislation for the greater good?

In general, respondents found the themes in the Draft Legislative Programme useful, as they showed what the aim of the programme was in broad terms. Many people agreed with them all in principle. In particular, people in the East Midlands felt that 'Handing power back to the people' and 'Making the most of your potential' were both important issues that the Government needed to address in order to make improvements for the greater good. In the North East and the North West, 'Making the most of your potential' was also highlighted as one of the most important themes to be pursued for the greater good. There was also support for this theme in the South East, where members of the public were keen to see the Government encouraging 'upskilling' in the labour market as a way for people to make the most of their potential.

Elsewhere, commentators were more critical of the Government's themes. In particular, some people in the West Midlands felt that they were helpful in principle, but that they did not address issues of implementation, transparency, or delivery. Some in the West Midlands also asked whether more legislation was what was needed for the greater good, suggesting that in fact reducing the number of laws would be a better way of helping people. In the North East, others were wary that themes could be no more than political rhetoric, and that it was difficult to see how change could take place on the ground if more concrete details were not pursued.

In Yorkshire and the Humber, respondents expressed their uncertainties as a desire to see the Draft Legislative Programme being presented in context.

Members of the public from a number of regions were pleased to see the themes addressing issues that they felt were close to the business community, and in particular to small businesses. However, it was again the detail of how these themes would be put into practice that occupied people's attention. For example, some people in the North East wanted to know what the business rate supplement Bill would contain, and how that would support the themes of the Programme.

In London, people were notably vocal in arguing that more focus should be placed on improving education, work and training opportunities, and on promoting the voice of young people.

6. Are there important issues which are not covered that you would like to see included? If so what are they?

Many people responded to this question in particular. In general, these responses listed specific issues relating to individuals or groups of individuals. However, other comments were far broader in scope. A sample of these issues is listed below:

- Access to public transport in rural areas
- Environmental issues, in particular climate change
- Join Bills up in a clearer manner
- Options for young people
- Tax breaks for community service
- Tougher immigration laws
- 15-17 year olds should be allowed in bars until a reasonable time, but not allowed to drink
- Leave teaching to teachers
- Break the cycle of underachieving in schools
- Stoke on Trent needs skilled jobs and local people trained to do them
- Cut fuel duty
- Simplify the tax system
- Scrap benefits system except for a very small minority of people
- Discourage antisocial behaviour
- Improve voter turnout
- Take account of regional needs
- Legislate for the fire service to provide a rescue response to floods. ***Government Response:*** *This is already being handled as part of the cross-Government National Flood Emergencies programme*
- Greater measures on economic stability with an international focus
- More to address crimes against businesses
- Equalise women's pensions with men's pensions
- Focus on higher education in the North East
- More focus on family relationships and involvement

7. Are there proposals which you think are unnecessary?

Broadly speaking, people were less concerned to highlight unnecessary proposals than they were to explain what they thought was missing from the Programme. However, some respondents felt that the following bills were not necessary:

- Heritage Protection Bill – measures felt to already be in place
- Communications Data Bill – unnecessary measure
- Education and Skills Bill – legislated on recently. ***Government Response:*** *The 2008-09 (4th) session Bill will build on the provisions in the Education and Skills Act which recently received Royal Assent. The intention is to put in place the necessary delivery mechanism to deliver the new duty to participate in education or training to the age of 18 that the recent Education and Skills Act introduced.*
- Business Rate Supplement Bill – concern at increasing regulatory burden

More specifically, the proposals in the Draft Legislative Programme were published before the draft NHS Constitution, meaning they were necessarily high level, leading some to question what it would cover. The need for proposals for elected representatives on police authorities was also questioned by some people. Other commentators were not convinced that anti-social behaviour orders were an efficient method of regulation, and asked whether more effective approaches could be developed. The Learning and Skills Council was highlighted by some as an important institution that should not be abolished. ***Government Response:*** *The Learning and Skills Council has helped drive significant progress towards its goal of improving the skills of England's young people and adults to create a workforce of world-class standard. To maintain this progress, the system needs to respond to new challenges and will require clear local leadership in every area. The Government wants local authorities to provide that leadership.*

Some people were opposed to more legislation in general, while others felt that housing targets were being imposed by legislation when in fact they were not needed. Finally, a small group were concerned by the Government's efforts to empower more people, arguing that this was a wasted effort and that it was just services that worked that were needed.

8. Further comments

In addition to responding to the specific questions in the Draft Legislative Programme, attendees at the events were also invited to make any other comments on it or on the issues discussed at the events. Across the country there were some common themes. In particular, respondents were concerned about the accessibility of the Draft Legislative Programme, and of the consultation exercise. It was broadly accepted that the wide range of consultation media and events this year meant that many more people were able to comment on the Programme than previously. One member of the public who is registered blind argued that Government documents, including the Draft Legislative Programme, were not sufficiently accessible for blind people. He urged the Government to make documents like this one available on tape or CD. A number of people across the North West raised concerns that the consultation focussed too heavily on the use of information technology in order to be able to contribute their views. Some people in the North East felt that the language in which some of the proposals were written was threatening, particularly in the case of the Citizenship, Immigration and Borders Bill. Critics in the South East were concerned that decisions were not being made on the basis of facts, and that more quantitative data should be evident in support of the bids.

Finally, the issue of empowering people was raised by some respondents. This was felt by these people to be a good thing, and that encouraging power sharing through the legislative process was a sensible way of supporting this aim.

9. What comments did people make on the content of these Bills?

The Banking Reform Bill was felt to be essential for the restoration of confidence in the global financial markets. It was recognised that the difficulties relating to the credit crunch need to be addressed, and rogue traders needed to be held to account. More broadly, the need to improve methods for dealing with irresponsible banks was felt to be of key importance.

The Education and Skills Bill attracted a wide range of comments, and was one of the central issues debated by attendees of the regional events. The right to time to train was largely felt to be a good measure. However, the fact that this right may impact on small to medium businesses was felt by some to be particularly pertinent. ***Government Response:*** *Time to train aims to help individuals to develop their skills and realise their full potential. That is why the right has been cast in very broad terms, so that employees can request time to undertake any training – whether nationally recognised qualifications, or shorter, more targeted, and unaccredited courses.*

While the right to request training was seen to be a good thing, concerns were raised about the type of training that employees would be allowed to take. Some respondents, for example at a selection of regional events in the North East, wanted reassurance that people would be free to choose training that would have a positive impact on them as individuals, and would not simply have to do training courses that would benefit their employers. It was recognised that self-employed people were often unable to take time out to train, and some people raised the possibility of reimbursing this group for doing training courses. Those in Northern Ireland felt that time to train provisions should apply there as well. ***Government Response:*** *The self-employed are eligible for Train to Gain funding, which includes public support for qualifications at level 2, apprenticeships and skills for life. These people cannot claim a contribution to wage costs for themselves, however, their employees may be eligible for contributions to wage costs, subject to the normal eligibility criteria. By 2010, the self-employed will also be able to use the universal adult advancement and careers service and a national system of Skills Accounts to help plan their training. The Northern Ireland Executive is considering the best way to take related provisions forward in Northern Ireland.*

Another key concern was that skills funding streams were driven from the centre by the adult skills agency and therefore that specific regional issues were not being properly addressed. Some attendees felt that the North East needed more discretion over initiatives designed to improve skills and that the role of skills in the Regional Funding Allocations and the development of the integrated regional strategy is unclear. Critics in this region also felt that skills analysis could improve as they felt that too many organisations were involved in the analysis process and that incoherence resulted. Attendees also asked for clarity on the nature of the interface between the adult skills agency, the Regional Delivery Authority and individual schemes. ***Government Response:*** *The Skills Funding Agency (SFA) will have a regional presence and will need to be able to work effectively with relevant partners to deliver Local Area Agreements (LAAs) and Multi Area Agreements (MAAs). They will also need to work effectively with Regional Skills Partnerships. Employment and Skills Boards – operating at sub regional level – will have a key role in articulating employer demand to which the SFA and providers will need to be able to respond. Regional Skills Partnerships will have a continuing role to play in ensuring that skills priorities sit within the wider regional strategy and as the mechanism for feeding through Regional Funding Advice on skills. The role of Regional Skills Partnerships will need to be refreshed to take into account the growing importance of the sub regional tier and the Machinery of Government changes.*

There was a mix of responses to the Government's proposals relating to 16-18 year olds. Transferring responsibilities relating to 16-18 education and training to local authorities in England, was felt to be important.

However, some people were concerned that the Government was making yet more changes to a system that was already struggling to cope with earlier alterations. ***Government Response:*** *The Government believes that to be serious about ensuring every 16-18 year old participates in some form of training or education, the right infrastructure must be in place, which the Bill will enable.* The detail of these proposals was requested by a number of attendees, who felt that, although this plan was sound in principle, the practical application of it may be lacking. *The White Paper 'Raising expectations: enabling the system to deliver' sets out the Governments proposals in detail. http://www.dcsf.gov.uk/publications/raisingexpectationswhitepaper/*

Apprenticeships were widely recognised as valuable, although in the North East a number of people felt that there would be a lack of young people willing to take them up. This was because of the poor image of certain careers resulting from apprenticeships such as those related to heavy industry and manufacturing sectors, and the fact that few talented young people were felt to want to pursue such careers. A wide-ranging Government plan to improve the image of apprenticeships and the resulting careers was suggested. ***Government Response:*** *The Government is working to strengthen apprenticeships and the National Apprenticeship Service will work with Connexions Advisers and schools to ensure that young people get better information about what apprenticeships are, and the opportunities that they provide. The image of apprenticeships has been negative for some time but now they offer young people the brightest prospects and employers a high quality, loyal workforce. The draft Apprenticeship Bill, which was published in July, sets out how these changes will be embedded and communicated.*

Tackling unemployment was seen as an important aim for the Government, and it was felt that there should be a focus on the provision of upskilling opportunities for the young unemployed in particular. ***Government Response:*** *The Government is seeking to address unemployment among young People by providing them with more education and training options. Beyond 18 the Bill will introduce a range of measures to increase young people's skills and employability, for example, National Apprenticeship Service, right to request time to train, improved education provision for those in juvenile custody and adult prisons.*

Further education establishments were felt to have missed out in this Bill, another area that could have been used to bolster the provision of opportunities for mature learners and adults. GCSEs were felt to have been over-emphasised as a measure of achievement in the education system, at the expense of 'value added' to pupils as they passed through the education system. ***Government Response:*** *The Government recognises that although not all young people will excel in GCSEs, they* *do have the ability to achieve in other formal education or training. That is why the Government is reforming and simplifying the qualifications system.*

Poorly performing schools were debated by a number of groups in the regions. Some people felt that these schools should simply be removed and replaced with something better, although the majority of people recognised that wider factors including the role of parents in children's education and addressing the 'lottery system' by which school places are assigned, need to be addressed. ***Government Response:*** *Improving the quality of schools for pupils and parents is essential if children and young people are to achieve their potential. Through this Bill the Government will strengthen the powers to intervene where schools require support, and improve the way in which parents can raise concerns about their child's school. School admissions will not be dealt with by this Bill.*

Vice Chancellors from universities in the North East felt that they needed to see more clarity in the Government's plans for the reform of 16-18 year olds' education. ***Government Response:*** *Plans were set out in the White Paper, Raising expectations: enabling the system to deliver.*

The Welfare Reform Bill elicited a divided response from those who commented. Some people felt that a harder line should be taken with those in receipt of benefits. To this end, skills assessments of those receiving benefits were seen as being a good measure to introduce. Some argued that benefits were too easy to get, and that the Government could try giving out vouchers instead of money. In contrast, others thought that it was wrong to make more stringent measures relating to benefits compulsory, as they felt that there were already sufficient pressures on this group of people and that more difficulties could be too much for the most disadvantaged. The poor image of the unemployed was felt to be one issue that the Government could actively influence for the better. These respondents argued that there should be more incentives to get people back into work, and that the way the legislation was phrased was very important. A sizeable minority of commentators argued that disabled people were not supported enough under the current system. These people welcomed the Government's efforts to give disabled people greater choice.

The review of sub-national economic development and regeneration formed a focus for many of the comments on the Community Empowerment, Housing and Economic Regeneration Bill. In addition to the comments on the economic development aspects of the Bill, respondents felt that the Government needed to give specific examples of the 'new tools' that they were proposing to supply to citizens. The practical implementation of community empowerment measures was felt to be lacking. ***Government Response:*** *Specific examples of community empowerment measures were set out in the Government consultation, 'Communities in Control', and in subsequent consultations. The renamed Local Democracy, Economic Development and Construction Bill will include a duty on local councils to respond to petitions.*

A second area of this Bill that attracted much debate was the Housing section. Broadly speaking, respondents wanted to see more affordable and rental housing, however a number of people criticized the Government's policy to build 3 million new homes by 2020. These people were not sure that this policy would have the desired effect at the local level. There was an underlying recognition that the difficulties associated with housing were not easy to solve, and that they were complex in their geographical distribution. People wanted to see plans that would take account of these local differences. Planning processes that were led at the local level were seen as one element of this development.

The Policing and Crime Reduction Bill was felt to be, broadly speaking, legislating in the correct area. An issue that drew particular attention from regional respondents was that of directly elected representatives on police authorities. Some people asked what electoral system would be used to achieve this, while others wanted to know what the cost of this measure would be. The Police were felt by some to be the wrong group to be targeted for this measure, as their position as experts was seen to be being challenged by this move. Two other issues were mentioned repeatedly by respondents in the regions. The first was the perceived need for a more visible police force, and for more police on the streets. The second was a concern for measures to reduce bureaucratic burdens in the police force, a measure that was felt to be threatening productivity. In particular, the speed of the police's response to crimes was noted as of particular importance, and a factor that could suffer if this measure was implemented. Others wanted to see the police force becoming more accountable on a local level, and within this context to be proactive and not reactive. This group of people supported the idea of reducing the burden of paperwork on the police force. The relationship between this legislation and the police in Northern Ireland was also raised. ***Government Response:*** *These proposals are to strengthen the link between the police and the public. The Casey Review found that local people are not clear who to hold to account for local policing and they expect a consistent standard of service anywhere in the country. The review showed that 67% of people would not know who to go to complain about bad policing. More recently the Association of Police Authorities commissioned IPSOS MORI poll showed that 55% supported the Government's proposals for direct election, All forces have already signed up to deliver the Policing Pledge – which will set a clear national entitlement for the public about what service they should receive as well* *as clear neighbourhood priorities for action. We have also dropped all top-down numerical targets for forces – save for one which measures whether the public are confident that their local concerns are being tackled – giving the police the freedom they have asked for. The Government proposes to build on this more visible, local accountability with direct elections to police authorities using the same electoral system currently used for General and Local elections. Where possible the elections will be combined. The cost of these proposals is affordable within the Home Office's budget and is not about cutting money from police funding. This proposal will not have any adverse impact on operational policing.*

Some attendees had strong reservations about the Business Rate Supplements Bill. These people felt that the Bill could damage the relationship between Local Authorities and businesses, and that it would damage small and medium-sized organisations. People were unsure whether the tax would result in an improvement in the environments of businesses, and therefore had reservations about the introduction of yet another supplementary tax. These people wanted to see the proceeds of the tax being ring-fenced, and a report on how they are spent being produced.

The Saving Gateway Bill prompted a variety of responses in the regions. Some people were very pleased to see this measure go ahead, and felt that it was deficient in that it did not go far enough in supporting the financially disadvantaged. There were some who argued that the very poorest people were unlikely to be able to afford to save anything, whether or not the Saving Gateway existed. Others felt that the Government should instead be focusing on the prevention of fraud, and on developing the skills and employment prospects of this group. These people felt that tax payers should not be asked to contribute to other people's savings. Throughout, there was a concern with the details of the process of qualifying for the Saving Gateway. ***Government Response:*** *The Government has consulted on the Saving Gateway and has listened to stakeholders and will aim to make the scheme as user-friendly as possible, in order to make the scheme accessible to those experiencing financial exclusion. The Government proposes to send an invitation to eligible individuals so as to ensure that qualifying for the scheme is as simple as possible for those who are eligible. The Government recognises that saving will be more difficult for those on lower incomes, so is introducing the Saving Gateway in order to give these individuals an additional incentive to do so.*

The Equality Bill, although received well by some groups, was seen to be vague and unenforceable by others. Some argued that this was an important Bill nonetheless, as it laid out an overarching system for equalities issues. In Northern Ireland, there were calls for the Government to keep working on its own Single Equality Bill regardless of this new legislation.

The NHS Reform Bill was included in the Draft Legislative Programme in advance of the publication of Lord Darzi's report (*High Quality Care for All)* and the draft NHS Constitution, both of which have been the subject of extensive, separate consultations. This meant the proposals in the Draft Legislative Programme were therefore necessarily high level and this is reflected in the responses. Some questioned whether the NHS Constitution was necessary. The Bill more generally was criticised for a perceived lack of action on the 'post code lottery'. Other concerns were that the Bill may take power away from medical experts, that mental health had been overlooked in the Bill, and that the proposals did not cover the means by which information could be shared between different health institutions. ***Government Response:*** *Both High Quality Care for All and the draft NHS Constitution have been subject to extensive consultation on their specific proposals. Lord Darzi's review included almost 100 events and captured the views of approximately 60,000 people – clinicians, patients and the wider public. Consultation on the NHS Constitution ran up to 17 October 2008; comments from the consultation on the Draft Legislative Programme are being considered as part of this process.*

The Citizenship, Immigration and Borders Bill also attracted a reasonable level of debate. Some people felt that it did not go far enough in restricting immigration, and that the Australian points system should be adopted in its entirety in the United Kingdom. These people also felt that immigrants should be made to learn English, and that more detailed criminal histories for them needed to be provided before they were allowed to enter the UK. Others felt that the citizenship test proposed by the Government was too complicated, and that the language of the Bill was threatening. Those from the business sector were wary that this bill could result in companies having to pay the Government a stipend to employ immigrant workers as is the case in Australia. The concept of a migration fund, to help manage the costs of migrants, was not welcomed. ***Government Response:*** *While migrants overall make a positive economic contribution they also use public services. We have recognised that, while we are consistently improving our systems for distributing resources to respond to patterns of migration, there can be transitional impacts on the provision of public services in communities which might be subject to rapid change. The fund, raised through increases to certain fees for immigration applications, will allow us to release limited amounts of money quickly and responsively.*

The Law Reform, Victims and Witnesses Bill, while seen as beneficial to witnesses, was felt to impact negatively on the accused. Some commentators wanted to see a separate court ruling as a pre-requisite to allowing a witness to give his or her evidence anonymously. ***Government Response:*** *The legislation will indeed provide for the court to grant a witness anonymity order, the decision will not rest with the police or prosecution.*

There were concerns raised over the Government's ability to keep data secure in relation to the Communications Data Bill, while measures in the Transport Security Bill were criticised as the security measures in airports were felt to already be too draconian. There was support for the Coroners and Death Certification Bill, and also for the 'protests in Parliament Square' provisions in the Constitutional Renewal Bill. Finally, the Marine and Coastal Access Bill and the Heritage Protection Bill were welcomed, although some felt that legislative time could be more usefully spent on other issues. Some people were concerned that these Bills would produce an extra burden for Local Authorities unless their long term benefits were articulated, and that sufficient resources to implement the laws were unlikely to be provided.

Parliamentary debates

The Prime Minister made a statement to the House of Commons on 14 May 2008 alongside the publication of the Draft Legislative Programme. He described the content of the programme and its overarching themes in detail and took questions during a short debate:

www.publications.parliament.uk/pa/cm200708/cmhansrd/cm080514/debtext/80514-0003.htm#08051449000004

The Leader of the Opposition was critical of the Banking Bill, as he felt that this reflected on the Government's management of the economy. He felt that much of the legislation in the 2007-08 (3rd) session was still struggling to pass through the Parliamentary process, and that the Government had run out of ideas.

The Leader of the Liberal Democrats argued moving the Draft Legislative Programme forward by two months was a way of creating some breathing space. He also argued that the Government was proposing too much new legislation, and pointed to the 65 Home Office Bills since 1997 and the 14 Health Bills in the last 10 years. Since 1997 the Home Office has passed 56 Bills. This compares with 68 Home Office Bills between 1990 and 1997, including 19 Bills in the 1996/7 parliamentary session.

Other Members of Parliament were concerned that debates on the Draft Legislative Programme and the Queen's Speech did not overlap and therefore waste time, and that issues of affordable housing, education, and the marine environment, amongst others, were adequately represented in the Programme.

The statement was repeated by the Leader of the House of Lords later the same day and a short debate in the House of Lords also followed:

http://www.publications.parliament.uk/pa/ld200708/ldhansrd/text/80514-0002.htm#08051462000008

Several Peers felt that the Draft Legislative Programme detracted from the Queen's Speech. Some felt that it made it harder, not easier, to see what legislation needed to be dropped in the coming programme. Others felt that the Government should concentrate on sorting out legislation in the current session of Parliament as opposed to making statements about the upcoming session, and that the statement on it had been composed in a rush. Other Lords defended the consultative purpose of the Draft Legislative Programme, and argued that it would allow effective public consultation. There was particular debate over the role of the Programme in addressing the issues relating to: provision for the very poor, acting on difficulties in the housing market and the banking sector, flexible working conditions for parents, shipping, bureaucracy in the police force, and reform of the House of Lords.

There was a further debate of around two and a half hours in the House of Commons on 26 June 2008 which was opened by the Leader of the House of Commons. The debate covered comments on a wide variety of the bills in the programme, including Banking Reform, Immigration, Communications Data, Constitutional Reform and Housing, which have been taken into account as part of the consultation process:

www.publications.parliament.uk/pa/cm200708/cmhansrd/cm080626/debtext/80626-0009.htm#column_535

FOUR – Online responses

In addition to the regional events, the Draft Legislative Programme was published on the Leader of the House of Commons website at www-commonsleader.gov.uk. People from across the UK were able to respond to the consultation online in three ways, by completing an online questionnaire, by commenting on individual bills in the programme and by suggesting ideas for new bills.

Online responses varied greatly in their length and content. Some correspondents answered one question, others answered several. Correspondents clearly valued the ability to engage with the consultation online.

Online questionnaire

The online questionnaire was completed by 198 respondents. Nine responses included positive comments about the Government's programme but the majority of responses to the online questionnaire were critical of the Government's plans. Many responses only commented on an individual policy area. These single policy comments most frequently noted the absence of particular issues from Bills. In addition to comments on the programme, many people used the questionnaire as an opportunity to communicate broader points, such as a range of comments expressing national pride.

Question 1 – Are the themes of the Draft Legislative Programme the right priorities for the Government to introduce for the greater good? If not, why not? What do you think the priorities should be?

Only five respondents to this question felt that the Government's priorities were the correct ones, although a further four felt that the themes under which the Draft Legislative Programme was organised were the right ones. One person felt that the theory supporting the legislation seemed good, but that delivery of the stated aims was also essential. The remaining respondents either felt that the Government had missed out some vital issues, or had got their priorities wrong. There were 28 responses about an English Parliament, while 11 called for greater Government transparency, a reduction in Government spending, less Parliamentary corruption or a shrinking of the public sector more generally. Seven people felt that the UK's membership of the European Union was bad for the country, and that we should withdraw from it. Seven respondents named the Communications Data Bill as a particularly bad idea, while four people felt that immigration provisions needed to be tightened further. Four people felt that there was already enough legislation and they didn't want to see any more.

Two other respondents wanted to see provisions for carers in the Programme, while three others felt that health issues should be central. Two more wanted the Government to focus on reducing fuel tax. Other issues that were suggested were: education issues including community service for everyone leaving college and a ban on selling school playing fields (8), the elderly and pensions (3), benefits for the disabled and unemployed (5), environment and renewables (6), the economy and responding to the financial crisis (4) and policing and crime prevention, including knife crime (5).

Individual respondents felt that the Government's priorities should be: defence, stopping the war in Iraq, protection from job losses due to moving production abroad, Human Rights, the right to protest without police permission, services for vulnerable adults, flexible working conditions for businesses, constitutional reform to prevent the break-up of the UK, reform of the House of Lords, defence of UK interests globally, improving housing provision, population control, building more prisons, heritage protection, elimination of discrimination, making the most of everyone's potential, avoiding interfering in people's lives, dropping the Welfare Reform Bill, inequalities in devolution policy, suspending Home Information Packs, a high-speed rail network, stop restricting asylum seekers' benefits, work towards fathers and grandparents' rights, decriminalise cannabis, restore capital punishment, lower taxes, stop drug companies making massive profits, account for Jewish burial practices, stop the decline of manufacturing industries, make sure that the Business Rate Supplements Bill doesn't damage Business Improvement Districts and remove the Education and Skills Bill.

Question 2 – Are the individual Bill proposals and non-legislative action in the Draft Legislative Programme the right issues on which the Government should focus its efforts? Are they relevant to you, your family and/or your community?

Many people either wrote entries that did not relate to this question, or did not answer it at all. Of those who did answer it, 39 gave a negative answer, 19 answered yes and 6 answered maybe. Three people felt that the Programme was relevant to themselves, their family and their community, three that it was relevant to themselves and their family only, two their family and their community only, and one just their community. Twelve people named particular Bill proposals as the right issues for the Government to focus on. These were:

- Equality Bill
- Housing provisions
- Saving Gateway Bill
- Banking Reform Bill
- Policing and Crime Reduction Bill
- Heritage Protection Bill
- Welfare Reform Bill
- NHS Constitution
- Marine and the Coastal Access Bill
- Coroners Bill
- Community Empowerment provisions
- Constitutional Renewal Bill

Question 3 – Do you think the Government is doing enough to improve legislation, to ensure it is necessary, to make it easier to understand and to fully consult? If not, what more do you think could be done in this area?

Only 11 people answered 'yes' to this question. In contrast, 104 people did not feel that the Government was doing enough to improve legislation, to ensure that it was necessary, to make it easier to understand and to fully consult.

44 respondents made comments relating to the improvement of legislation. Of these, 18 related to an English Parliament, while four wanted the UK to leave the European Union. Five people felt that the effective implementation of laws was what the Government needed to focus on. Two people wanted the Government to engage in more debate with the public over the legislative programme, and give people more feedback, while one person wanted to see the detail of Bills being discussed more widely. Other people wanted the Government to: support fathers and grandfathers, cut the Communications Data Bill, leave the NHS alone, abolish Home Information Packs, unfreeze pensions, stop discrimination against young single mothers, develop effective leaders, restrict immigration, care more for the elderly, ensure the Police to do more to protect citizens, have Government in the regions as opposed to in Westminster, and inform the public on what oil and gas money is being spent on.

19 people did not feel that existing legislation that already existed and that which was proposed in the Draft Legislative Programme was necessary. Of these people, some went further and argued that there was also a surplus of Government bureaucracy and red tape and that this needed to be reduced.

10 respondents specifically criticised the degree to which legislation was easily understandable. These people felt that the Government was poor at explaining things and that simple laws written in plain English were what was needed. One person felt that the website browser that they were using was not accessible enough.

18 people made comments relating to the inadequacies of the Government's consultation process. A number of these people wanted consultations to be aimed at different groups in society and for them to be consulted more effectively. These groups included disabled people, 14-19 year olds, experts, non-experts, and citizens via their constituency MPs. Some argued that consultations should be longer, while others felt that consultations were a waste of time. Finally, seven people wanted more consultations, and for the Government to act on what people said.

Question 4 – Are there important issues which are not covered by the Draft Legislative Programme that you would like to see included? If so what are these?

A total of 168 responses were submitted to this question and in total 67 issues were highlighted. The issue of an English Parliament was raised by 23 people, and 9 raised issues about the funding arrangements for the devolved administrations. 12 people made comments relating to UK's membership of the European Union, and to immigration. Of these comments, 8 argued that we should have a referendum on Europe or restrict immigration, while 4 argued that we should play a greater role in European affairs. 9 respondents were keen to see more environmentally aware legislation, including laws to limit the use of 4x4s, and reduce carbon emissions, while 8 people wanted to see improvements to the tax system and to the accountability of local authorities. A further 8 respondents asked for improvements to the position of pensioners in society, while three people felt that more needed to be done to promote further education. Two further respondents wanted to see a review of the use of force in Iraq and Afghanistan, while two others wanted to see payments being made to informal carers.

Other issues which were proposed included:

- Compulsory work for the unemployed
- Cycle tracks on all roads
- Improved armed forces pensions

- Better energy security
- Reduced youth street crime
- Improved prisons
- Tougher prison sentences
- Response to peak oil prices
- Reduction in petrol prices
- Cap on utility prices
- Response to anti-social behaviour
- More respect from children to elders
- National service
- Improved postal system
- Sufficient indigenous food production
- Fathers and grandparents' rights
- Legalised cannabis
- Equality Act to apply to all minority groups
- Support for local pub community life
- Ban on trans-fats
- Less red tape
- Account for Jewish interests in autopsies
- Metrication of speed signs
- Action against 'consumer culture'
- Safeguard vulnerable adults in primary legislation
- Remove the right to collective worship in schools
- Control the use of DNA
- Better special needs education
- Regeneration of run down commercial sectors
- Continued support for freedom of speech legislation
- Help for those in rural areas

Question 5 – Are there proposals included in the Draft Legislative Programme which you think are unnecessary? If so what are these and why are they unnecessary? Is the Government acting on the issues that matter to people?

Many people either did not answer this question, or wrote responses that were not related to it. Of those who did respond to the question, 26 did not think there were unnecessary proposals in the Draft Legislative Programme. 69 people did think some proposals were not needed, while 5 people were not sure.

Of those people who thought that proposals were unnecessary, 43 named specific bills or issues. These included:

- Immigration provisions (3 people)
- Saving Gateway Bill (2 people)
- Communications Data Bill (2 people)
- Equality Bill (2 people)
- Community Empowerment, Housing and Economic Regeneration Bill (2 people)
- Welfare Reform Bill (2 people)
- Education and Skills Bill (4 people)
- Business Rate Supplements Bill
- Banking Reform Bill
- More taxes
- The powers of the Attorney General
- Local Planning provisions
- Proposed changes to the Tenants Association
- Alterations to incapacity benefit
- Withholding hospital funding from underperforming institutions
- Bin tax proposals
- Public transport proposals
- Environmental provisions
- Giving the Civil Service statutory status
- Stealth taxes
- Benefits for old people

- Right of underprivileged
- Elected police boards
- Shared ownership of property policies
- Health legislation

Online Bill comments

General Comments

542 comments were made on specific Bills. While the overall number of people commenting on specific Bills was encouraging, the number making points about each particular Bill was often small. For example, less than 10 people commented on 4 of the 18 Bills.

Specific Comments

Equality Bill – 107 comments
This Bill received the most individual comments. Some comments were positive, but the majority highlighted areas of equality policy which they felt needed to be expanded. In particular, the majority of comments noted that trans people were not being treated fairly by the Bill. Respondents keen to support the rights of trans people, particularly those who had not had gender reassignment surgery, wanted to see stronger legislative provisions to support this group. Some people did not want positive discrimination of women in politics, although these comments were in the minority. ***Government Response:*** *This comment is taken to apply to the use of women-only shortlists, the use of which the Bill will extend to 2030, partly as a means of encouraging an increase in the proportion of women MPs, which is currently just over 19% of the total.*

Constitutional Renewal Bill – 92 comments
The Reform of the House of Lords, promised by the Government, was felt by some to have been side-tracked. Further reforms were notably absent from this Bill, a fact that was highlighted in comments on this Bill. Some people were pleased that provisions in this Bill would alter the right to protest outside Parliament.

Communications Data Bill – 68 comments
Most commentators were strongly critical of this Bill. They felt that it was another erosion of public freedoms, and that the Government had no right to store data in the way. Some people suggested that this Bill was similar to the Government's plans for identity cards, and that similar arguments existed to the two policies. A number of comments highlighted the Government's recent inability to keep large databases

secure, arguing that allowing another massive database to be created and held was clearly not sensible. Some people felt that there should be a Bill that did the opposite to this one and reinforced people's privacy instead of reducing it. ***Government Response:*** *Contrary to press reporting, there are no plans to collect and keep the content of communications. Communications data – which is the who, where and when of a communication but not the content – is a vital tool in law enforcement and public protection. Traditionally, Communications Service Providers have kept this data for business purposes such as billing. The Regulation of Investigatory Powers Act 2000 set out a framework covering access to data to ensure that the police and intelligence agencies could only get access to data when it was proportionate and necessary to do so. However, the development of the potential of the internet and internet technology by the communications industry has led to an explosion in the number of communications, and the different ways that people communicate. These developments, which are driven by technological change, will increasingly undermine the Government's current capability to obtain communications data and use it to protect the public. The Government will be consulting early in 2009 on how to maintain this vital source of intelligence and evidence, in the face of the impact of changing technology. This consultation will set out the emerging problem, the important capability gaps that need to be addressed and to look at the possible solutions, seeking views. It will also look at what safeguards would be needed, in addition to the many in place already, to provide a solid legal framework that protects civil liberties.*

NHS Reform Bill – 55 comments

The most often repeated comment on the NHS Reform Bill was that carers and unpaid partners were under-represented by existing legislation. These comments argued that carers were saving the Government large amounts of money by shouldering the task of caring for many elderly and infirm people in society, and keeping them out of expensive hospital beds. Some people felt that health inequalities needed to be addressed, while others were critical of a perceived growth in the number of bureaucrats in the NHS. ***Government Response:*** *Since the publication of the Draft Legislative Programme, the Government has published Lord Darzi's report 'High Quality Care for All', along with a draft NHS Constitution. The draft Constitution sets out the principles on which the NHS is based, including: its commitment to equality and access to all; the need for services to reflect the needs and preferences of patients, their families and carers; and a commitment to value for taxpayers' money and the effective and fair use of finite resources. 'High Quality Care for All' gives a commitment to explore the potential of personal budgets, and in particular to legislate to enable the piloting of direct payments for health services, where this makes most sense for individual patients. The personal health budgets programme is working actively in partnership with the NHS, local authority, carers and patient groups.*

Welfare Reform Bill – 37 comments

Comments on this Bill were wide-ranging, running from people who felt that the disabled were not being supported enough, to those who felt that the unemployed were made to feel worthless in society, and that the Government should do something to address this issue.

Citizenship, Immigration and Borders Bill – 32 comments

Most of the people who commented on this Bill wanted to see immigration laws being tightened. A number of people felt that immigrants and asylum seekers should be treated more severely, and that they should be made to learn English language and culture. Some others were keen to see immigration laws becoming less discriminatory towards immigrants. Others agreed with these comments, feeling that those with less education could be discriminated against by the existing system. ***Government Response:*** *The Citizenship, Immigration and Borders Bill was included in the Draft Legislative Programme in advance of the publication of the Draft (partial) Immigration and Citizenship Bill. This was published on 14 July 2008 and sets out proposals for a fundamental overhaul of the law in this area, replacing all current immigration laws. The new law could mean stronger borders, be easier for the UK Borders Agency to enforce and ensure newcomers earn the right to stay by learning English, paying taxes and obeying the law. The Bill is receiving pre-legislative scrutiny by the Home Affairs Select Committee and the Government continues to develop it in an open and collaborative manner.*

Education and Skills Bill – 22 comments

Some commentators felt that this Bill could be an effective tool to ensure that parents have their say to ensure that their children get a good education. However, most of the comments outlined areas of schools policy that they felt had been eroded over the past decades. These areas included: discipline, options for 16 and 17 year olds, underachievement in Maths and the support of mature students. ***Government Response:*** *The Bill will improve the way in which parental complaints and concerns are dealt with by their child's school. It would also strengthen collaboration between schools, giving them the powers they need to improve standards of behaviour, and enable the delivery system to provide 16-18 year olds with appropriate education or training.*

Community Empowerment, Housing and Economic Regeneration Bill – 21 comments

Comments on this Bill focused on the level to which power should be devolved to local communities. Some people felt that this Bill did not go far enough, and that parish councillors, for example, were not empowered by it. Others felt that regional investments should be driven by local needs, and that individuals should be consulted on actions in their particular areas. Finally, one person felt that the rights of the tenant should be addressed by the Bill. ***Government Response:*** *Legislation to* *strengthen the role of Local Authorities in economic development should help deliver more local-led investment decisions. The Bill would also include the duty to promote democracy, and an 'extended duty to involve,' designed to help ensure that citizens can influence decisions in their areas. The Bill would also include legislation on a National Tenant Voice.*

<u>Law Reform, Victims and Witnesses Bill – 18 comments</u>
A number of observations related to sentencing policy ranging from the need for mandatory life sentences in murder cases, to support for restorative justice in cases of criminal damage. There was support for proposals to stop convicted criminals profiting from publications about their crimes and for strengthening the Witness Charter by enshrining it as a code, along similar lines to the Victims Code, to give equality to all people coming into contact with the justice system.

<u>Saving Gateway Bill – 15 comments</u>
A number of critics felt that taxes should not be spent on encouraging those on benefits to save. There was a perception that public trust in the Government was low and that the gains of this plan could be outweighed by the administrative costs associated with it. A number of people expressed the opinion that the welfare state was meant to provide a financial safety net as opposed to savings. Some commentators argued that money should instead be spent on encouraging credit unions, increasing the old age pension or reducing tax on savings interest instead.

<u>Coroners and Death Certification Bill – 14 comments</u>
Comments on this Bill supported the rights of the bereaved. To this end, people argued that the Bill had to address: waiting times for inquests, the need for coroners to monitor the system of care for vulnerable people which may be a contributory factor in their death, and 'Coroners Removal' contracts which were perceived as anti-competitive and to the detriment of bereaved families. More generally, respondents felt that coroners needed to be more accountable. ***Government Response:*** *These comments reinforced the responses to the consultation on the Draft Charter for the Bereaved, published in June 2008 (http://www.justice.gov.uk/docs/draft-charter-bereaved.pdf). The provisions include the role of Chief Coroner, who will be able to address concerns about specific types of death and national coronial practices and standards.*

<u>Banking Reform Bill – 13 comments</u>
Commentators were keen to see savings protection rates increased, and also for bankers to be punished for risk-taking strategies. One person argued that clearing house procedures needed to be updated. ***Government Response:*** *During the recent period of financial turbulence, the Authorities have taken timely and decisive action to*

protect depositors and savers. From 7 October 2008, the Financial Services Authority (FSA) has increased the compensation limit on deposits with banks, building societies and credit unions from £35,000 to £50,000. In addition, the Chairman of the FSA, Lord Turner, at the request of the Chancellor, will be conducting a review which will make recommendations for reforming UK and international approaches to regulation, to ensure the future stability of the UK banking system. The FSA is also conducting a review of remuneration practices, and has written to the Chief Executives of major banks to indicate the need for better alignment between executive remuneration and incentives for long term performance. The Authority has indicated that it will take UK firms' performance against good principles of remuneration policy into account when they review firms' overall risk. The FSA intends to issue a report on remuneration policy early in the New Year.

The Banking Bill will formalise the role of the Bank of England in the oversight of payment systems. This includes those payment systems embedded within recognised clearing houses and recognised investment exchanges. However, the FSA will continue to regulate investment exchanges and clearing houses.

Marine and Coastal Access Bill – 12 comments

A notable group of commentators felt that it was important that this Bill built on the rights of walkers granted in the Countryside and Rights of Way Act (2000), and extended these rights to horse riders in the countryside. Others were concerned that Marine reserves needed to be set up to protect coastal waters and that hydrographic data needed to be made available to the public without charge. ***Government Response:*** *These issues also arose in the pre-legislative scrutiny and public consultation on the Draft Marine Bill. The full Government response was published on 25 September 2008 and can be found at: http://www.official-documents.gov.uk/document/cm74/7422/7422.pdf.*

Policing and Crime Reduction Bill – 9 comments

While some commentators argued that police time could be saved by employing well-qualified clerks to check license number plates, and run other more menial policing tasks, others felt that the increased number of community police, and the consequent reduction of the number of fully qualified police, had eroded the service provided by forces. ***Government Response:*** *There has been an increased use by police forces of staff in roles not requiring the full powers of a police officer. These include, for example, in investigation and detention roles as well as in administrative or back office type functions. The Policing Green Paper contains a number of measures designed to ensure that, in allocating tasks to appropriately skilled and qualified staff, forces and authorities provide the highest quality of service to the public. A major workforce inspection in 2010 will hold forces and authorities to account in ensuring they have an appropriate mix of officers and staff to provide the best possible service to the public.*

The introduction of Police Community Support Officers has not resulted in a reduction in police officers. Police officer numbers are at a historically high level and have increased by over 14,000 since 1997. The 16,000 Police Community Support Officers are a valuable addition to the policing family and provide a vital part of neighbourhood policing teams with their focus on high visibility reassurance policing and community engagement.

Heritage Protection Bill – 9 comments
Comments on this Bill were critical of its scope, and suggested that the ability of local authorities to sell off conservation areas was not sufficiently controlled.

Business Rate Supplements Bill – 8 comments
The key concerns included the possible impact of the Bill on Business Improvement Districts; that district councils would be better placed to levy the supplement; and that local authorities should have more control over how the supplement will work. Others raised the concern that the Bill may make some bankrupt as it was another burden on small to medium sized businesses, and they felt that it was rather arbitrary in its application.

Geneva Conventions and United Nations Personnel Bill – 6 comments
Comments on this Bill were broadly supportive. One person asked whether the UN Laissez-Passer passport would be recognised by this Bill for passing across borders. ***Government Response:*** *The Bill would allow the UK to accede to the Optional Protocol to the Convention on the Safety of United Nations Personnel. The Protocol does not affect the United Nations Laissez-Passer passport. The Laissez-Passer passport already allows the holder to travel to the United Kingdom on official business without a national passport or entry clearance. However, when holders travel to the UK for any other reason, they should use their national passports (and visas will be required by visa nationals).*

Transport Security Bill – 4 comments
These few comments were divided over whether this Bill was a good or bad idea. One critic felt that the Bill would not achieve anything that was not already covered by existing legislation.

Make your own Bill

General Comments

Eleven people suggested ideas for new Bills. These suggestions ranged in breadth from very wide-reaching suggestions that, for example, called for greater accountability in all Local Government dealings, or for public transport companies, to more targeted offerings such as proposals to more severely punish those carrying knives.

The function allowing people to suggest new Bills will be kept on the Leader of the House of Commons' website year-round. This means that permanently members of the public will have a facility to make comments relating to the process of making legislation regardless of whether there is a particular consultation occurring or not.

Suggested Bills

The titles of the suggested Bills are listed below with a brief description of what the people who proposed them felt that they should do:

Equality for people without children – Having children is a lifestyle choice, and those without children should have the equal opportunity to take sabbaticals etc for whatever reason.

Noise reduction – Legislate against the use of noisy equipment.

Public safety – Increase punishment for knife carriers.

Family unit – Reinstate the family as the basic unit of society.

Housing benefits fair deal for all – When made redundant or unemployed, home owners should not be penalised for having a private mortgage.

Public transport – Public transport to be more accountable.

Compulsory working act – Make it a legal requirement to be in work if 18-21 with no other (acceptable) employment.

Separation of government and religion – Split ethics and morality.

Independent living – Promote and protect an independent life for those with physical and especially sensory disabilities.

Transport infrastructure (funding) – Shift primary transport from road to rail.

Responsible authority – Make Local Authorities more accountable.

FIVE – Postal responses

In recognition of the fact that not everyone has access to the internet, responses to the consultation were also sought by post. As well as maintaining a freepost address which anyone could use to register their comments on the Draft Legislative Programme without charge, 30,000 leaflets were distributed to public libraries. The purpose of the leaflets was to increase the knowledge of the general public about the draft programme. In addition it contained a tear-off section that could be returned by post to the Government for consideration. Some organisations and individuals chose to send their comments to the Government independently.

The Secretaries of State for Wales, Scotland and Northern Ireland wrote to key stakeholders drawing their attention to the consultation, and encouraging people to complete the online responses. This generated a number of written and online responses.

Finally, ePolitix.com, an independent political research organisation, was requested by the Leader of the House of Commons to provide a Parliamentary briefing paper to be fed formally into the consultation on the Draft Legislative Programme. The 21 organisations who responded in this briefing paper commented on 14 of the 18 draft Bills.

Freepost responses/postal responses

General Comments

The majority of the 51 responses received by letter came from organisations and companies which were commenting with reference to their official positions on the subjects that the legislation related to. The comments received in this format were often more detailed and in-depth than those from other postal sources or from internet sources.

As a consequence of these people not being constrained by particular questions, often the responses that were received focused more heavily on issues close to the organisation or individual, as opposed to those specifically related to the Bills.

Comments by companies and organisations

37 organisations responded by letter to the consultation. These comments were overwhelmingly organised according to each Bill, although some comments asked to see in more detail how the Programme would dovetail with the interests of the devolved administration.

A number of organisations supported the Business Rate Supplements Bill, although some organisations were concerned that the extra tax provisions would impact on them more strongly than other sectors of society. Kingston Town Centre Management was worried that they had 338 businesses over the £50,000 taxable threshold, and so would be affected severely by the tax. They suggested that a Business Rate Supplements offset scheme could be introduced in towns where businesses invest in a Business Improvement District. In the East of England, it was felt that the ring-fencing of this tax needed to be properly enforced. Others shared the concerns of Kingston Town Centre Management about its potential impact on medium-sized businesses.

Comments on the Education and Skills Bill were received from five different organisations. While apprenticeships were broadly welcomed, commentators felt that it was very important that employers were 'bought in' to the training process. ***Government Response:*** *The Government agrees, which is why it is committed to working closely with stakeholders throughout.*

Some people felt that the needs of older workers were unlikely to be taken into account, despite these new laws. One organisation felt that there was a lack of transparent market for the use of funding, and therefore that moving towards a demand-driven system was essential.

The Equality Bill attracted significant interest from a range of organisations. Several commentators were very pleased to see this Bill in the Draft Legislative Programme. The kite-mark for businesses was felt to be particularly useful, as were efforts to improve the measurement of progress in the equality field. While the Bill was widely supported, some commentators felt that it did not go far enough in legislating for an equal society. In particular, it failed to harmonise the law on all issues, and did not protect those who felt that they had a trans identity unless they had undergone gender reassignment surgery. One organisation suggested that the Government keep open the options of introducing equal pay audits in the future, better protection for pregnant workers, developing government procurement provisions so that only companies with a good track record in gender equality are chosen, and having equality representatives with statutory protection and paid time off, and more effective legal redress. Finally, one organisation believed that the Government was using this Bill to impose ideological views on society in regard to sexual relationships, which they felt was wrong, and wanted to see more emphasis on religious freedoms.

The Welfare Reform Bill was widely welcomed by organisational respondents, who liked the idea of modernising and simplifying the benefit system. The current system was felt to be inflexible and not effective. However, the Tax Credits system, which overpaid many people and then demanded the extra money back, was cited as a process that had not been effective and had engendered distrust of the welfare system. One organisation felt that the Government had a duty to give positive benefits to married families. Finally, one organisation argued that it was inappropriate to increase requirement on clients over 50 unless a range of pre-conditions were met, particularly in relation to the delivery of tailored support to these people.

The East of England Development Agency commented on the Citizenship, Immigration and Borders Bill, which, they were concerned, was not consistent with the ambition stated in the East of England Regional Economic Strategy of attracting and retaining talent. They felt that the 'Improving public services' theme implied a narrow impacts focus, that immigration is a 'problem' to be controlled (poor use of language), that the 'migration fund' implies that skilled migrants were imposing a cost on the country, and believed that points-based systems were slow to respond to circumstances and market conditions. The Association of Chief Police Officers in Wales asked that the Welsh Language Act be taken into account when requiring immigrants to learn English when in the UK.

The Community Empowerment, Housing and Regeneration Bill also attracted significant comment. Fewer people expressed their support for this Bill, although some people particularly welcomed the provisions on housing. However, these provisions were not felt to have gone far enough in helping first time buyers to get on to the housing ladder by removing financial hurdles to their doing this. Additionally, some called for more measures from the Government to move away from subsidised housing. One argued that the Bill in general had been written from an English perspective and that there was scope to reduce crime and antisocial behaviour by mandating that crime prevention be incorporated into new housing developments. Others were concerned that an overemphasis on financial issues in the Bill would detract from its aim of empowering people and would eclipse environmental aims. A vocal few commentators also argued that a strategic regional approach should be pursued more closely in this Bill.

The Royal College of Nursing was clear in stating that it was firmly committed to an NHS which is tax funded, universally provided, and free at the point of need. They wanted to see rights and responsibilities enshrined in an NHS Constitution and for appropriate resources to be provided to support this. Other commentators noted that in 1991 the Patient's Charter had also aimed to provide similar results, but in their view had failed. There was a perceived imbalance between general managers and clinical leaders within hospitals, which some organisations wanted to see addressed in legislation, while others saw this Bill as an opportunity to recognise old people and their needs.

Two organisations commented on the Coroners and Death Certificates Bill. While the safeguards that it contained were welcomed, some commentators wanted to see coroners' work focusing on the prevention of future deaths, strengthening the role of relatives, and on reforming the death certification scheme more generally. ***Government Response:*** *The Government agrees with these points, all of which will be addressed in the Coroners and Justice Bill. Indeed, following the consultation on the draft Coroners Bill the Government announced, in March 2006, a number of changes to the Bill along these lines can be found at http://www.justice.gov.uk/docs/coroners-bill-changes.pdf.*

One organisation commented on the Heritage Protection Bill, which they were generally pleased with, but had two concerns. Firstly, they felt that the special local interest designation will not mean inclusion in the Heritage Register for England and Wales, and secondly, that appeals against decisions on 'heritage asset consents', that is, changes to listed building can be made by delegated powers by local member review boards, who are unlikely to be objective.

Support was also expressed for the Marine and Coastal Access Bill and the Draft Floods and Water Bill. However, one organisation felt that the Policing and Crime Reduction Bill had been drafted from an English perspective and that it failed to address the very different local government situation that exited in Wales.

One organisation called for a comprehensive national databank of health and injury statistics, while there were also calls for more legislation on lighthouses and rural access to post offices.

Comments by members of the public

Fourteen members of the public posted their comments to the Government.

Few of these comments related to particular Bills. However, there were expressions of support for the Equality Bill and the Education and Skills Bill. However, one person felt that the Policing and Crime Reduction Bill needed to legislate for a policing system that reflected the localised system which currently exists. One respondent was particularly keen to see the Geneva Conventions and United Nations Personnel Bill reach Royal Assent, as they felt that the international legislation that it would enact should not be put off endlessly. The same respondent also agreed with the Constitutional Renewal Bill's aim to keep the Attorney General as the Government's chief legal advisor.

Two commentators felt that the website needed to be more user-friendly, while others wanted to see Northern Irish and Scottish bank notes removed from circulation, charities to have their statuses altered, and improvements in Burnley. ***Government Response:*** *The Government is protecting Northern Irish and Scottish bank notes in legislation as part of the Banking Bill.*

Leaflet responses

General Comments

Thirty tear-off slips from the leaflet were received. These slips included four questions, the responses to which are summarised below.

1. **Overall, what do you think about the themes, bills and other actions outlined in the Draft Legislative Programme? How much do they match your own priorities for what you think the Government should be doing?**

A range of responses were given to this question, ranging from 'excellent' to 'useless'. It was clear from the responses to the regional events that a significant number of people felt that the themes were useful in pointing out the purpose of the Programme. However, people's responses to individual bills were very different to their responses to themes, and so it is possible that the mixed response to this question reflected this ambiguity. Several of the 30 respondents felt that they had 'no confidence' in the Government's legislative actions, and that, despite the appearance of a different, more transparent approach to legislation, the Government was in fact delivering more of the same in terms of legislation.

While some commentators felt that the Government's priorities did not match their own, there were few suggestions for what the Government should be doing instead. One person felt that people wanted efficient services and not power, while a second person wanted to see tighter immigration policy.

2. Looking at the themes on pages 2 and 3, which of them should the Government focus on in the year ahead?

The majority of responses to this question named individual Bills as the correct focal points for Government action, as opposed to themes. Some people named aims that were neither Bills nor themes. The following foci were suggested:

- Welfare Reform
- Policing and Crime Reduction
- Education and Skills
- Citizenship and Immigration
- NHS Reform
- Saving Gateway
- Economic Stability
- Antisocial Behaviour
- Flexible working hours
- Public sector services
- Time off to train

3. Are there any proposals in the Draft Legislative Programme which you believe are unnecessary?

Four of the thirty people who responded by leaflet felt that there were no unnecessary proposals in the Programme, while three people felt that 'most of them' were unnecessary. While individual respondents named the Banking Reform Bill, the Welfare Reform Bill, the Education and Skills Bill, the Immigration provisions, the NHS Constitution, and further rights for women as unnecessary, four additional commentators felt that the Saving Gateway Bill was surplus to requirements. Five people felt that the right to time off to train did not need to be legislated for, while two more people wanted to see proposals supporting agency workers removed.

4. Are there important issues which are not covered by the Draft Legislative Programme that you would like to see included?

Everyone who responded by leaflet had suggestions for important issues that had been missed from the Draft Legislative Programme. The three most often mentioned issues were calls for UK's withdrawal from the European Union, greater focus on environmental issues and improvements to the public transport infrastructure. While a number of suggestions focused on making the Government's response to crime, antisocial behaviour, immigration and terrorism more stringent, others wanted to see improvements in social services, devolution, supporting the elderly, retraining the over 50s, employment, taxation, the accountability of the police force and Members of the European Parliament, affordable rents and cheap houses, higher education, low food and petrol costs and airport expansion.

e-Politix

General Comments

The organisation e-Politix aims to encourage better communication between politicians and the public. It provides a range of internet-based services, including home pages for MPs, blogs, news and interview summaries.

The organisation was in an excellent position to co-ordinate the responses of a range of stakeholders on the Draft Legislative Programme. The 40 comments from 21 organisations referred to the following Bills:

- Banking Reform Bill
- Business Rate Supplements Bill
- Draft Civil Law Reform Bill
- Community Empowerment, Housing and Economic Regeneration Bill
- Coroners and Death Certification Bill
- Education and Skills Bill
- Equality Bill
- Draft Floods and Water Bill
- Heritage Protection Bill
- Marine and Coastal Access Bill
- NHS Reform Bill
- Saving Gateway Bill
- Transport Security Bill
- Welfare Reform Bill

The Association of British Insurers felt that the Banking Reform Bill was a sensible legislative step, but that the first consultation on this issue did not prove the case for the 'special resolution regime'. Therefore, they felt that a higher level of deposit protection and pre-funding a deposit protection scheme are not justified.

Both the Federation of Small Businesses and the Royal Institute of Chartered Surveyors are concerned about the Business Rate Supplements Bill. They feel that this Bill will allow top tier local authorities to charge businesses a levy on top of non domestic rates currently paid and, therefore, work must be done to make sure this is not just another tax burden on businesses.

The Association of Personal Injury Lawyers welcomed the Draft Civil Reform Bill. They hope that it will focus on full and fair compensation, especially in relation to compensation for pain, suffering and loss of amenity. They also welcome extending the list of categories of those who can claim financial losses following wrongful death, and they feel that the reward limit is not high enough, and that rules for claims relating to 'long tail' diseases and against defunct companies need to be altered.

Several organisations commented on the Community Empowerment, Housing and Economic Regeneration Bill. The majority of comments were relating to the housing provisions in the Bill, which were broadly welcomed and in particular supported if they moved towards zero-carbon housing by 2016. The Council of Mortgage Lenders was keen to welcome help from the Government for first time buyers, as well as a review of sale-and-leaseback schemes. Other organisations felt that the Government's lack of investment in housing stock was short-sighted and that it will be costly in health terms in the long run. Elsewhere, respondents felt that the Bill in fact centralised power as opposed to devolved it, while Age Concern wanted to see old people at risk of social exclusion being accounted for in more detail by the legislation.

One organisation commented on the Coroners and Death Certification Bill. They argued that the current system is archaic and needs review. Although there was much in the bill to support, including full-time coroner posts and the Coroners (Amendment) Rules 2008, they felt that no emphasis was put on the right to legal advice and representation for bereaved families. They also raised concerns that the new system will be locally as opposed to centrally funded.

The Education and Skills Bill attracted comments from a significant number of respondents. Teachers' and Lecturers' organisations felt that the Government was making some sensible moves in terms of its legislation on education. In particular, the focus on those who are failing in the current system was accurate. However, the Government's attempts to cut the number of these schools was not felt to be the right approach, and that instead it should work to recognise that the unbalanced intake of pupils from different backgrounds was a more important factor. Relating to this point were arguments that the Government should encourage less top down accountability and more local level development, and those that pointed to the detail of proposals, as opposed to the high level theory behind them, as the most important issues. For example, an unhealthy relationship between some schools and their local authorities was highlighted as one issue that needed to be addressed. ***Government Response:*** *The Government is not seeking to cut the number of schools. Rather it wants to ensure that all schools provide children and young people with the best possible education. That is why this Bill will strengthen the powers to intervene where schools require support. One way in which the Bill will seek to promote better co-ordination and accountability locally is by giving schools a greater role within the Children's Trust – thus ensuring their views are fully reflected in the Trust's work.*

Other organisations were more interested in the training provisions in this Bill, in particular the 'right to request' time for training, which they felt was potentially dangerous if in practice it became a compulsion on small businesses later on. Finally, Age Concern again asked whether this legislation would be used to remove age barriers in adult skills entitlements and ensure that everyone can benefit from skills training. ***Government Response:*** *The right to request time to train away from core duties to undertake training would apply to all employees.*

Eight organisations commented on the Equality Bill, the most comments in the e-Politix report on any Bill. A number of these comments were positive, notably from the Trade Union Congress and the Equality and Human Rights Commission. The fact that the Bill will simplify and clarify legislation and bring it together was felt to be very positive. However, a note of caution was sounded on the enforcement of this Bill, as respondents were clear that without fair implementation the Bill could have little real impact. In particular, measures on positive action were felt to be potentially dangerous if their use was not carefully controlled. People felt that it was the basic aim of equal rights that was the most important, and that in pursuing this aim the Government needed to remember the elderly and the mentally infirm.

Three organisations welcomed the provisions contained in the Heritage Protection Bill, which they felt would create a more accountable heritage protection system and would encourage greater stakeholder involvement in heritage protection. Again, it was the implementation of the Bill that was felt to be the most important factor to continue to pursue.

While the three comments received on the Marine and Coastal Access Bill welcomed it, the Association of British Insurers wanted to see a long-term flood management strategy in the Draft Floods and Water Bill. ***Government Response:*** *It is intended that this will be made possible by the draft Bill.*

Elsewhere, respondents felt that the help to home owners contained in the Saving Gateway Bill would certainly be outweighed by market conditions, that there needed to be a greater occupational health element in the NHS Reform Bill, that the policing costs in the Transport Security Bill were likely to be handed on to the consumer, that support for the over-50s would not be appropriate to their needs, and that the Health and Safety at Work Act 1974 should be amended to impose statutory health and safety duties on company directors.

SIX – Links to departmental consultations

In addition to the consultation on the Draft Legislative Programme some departments held separate consultations on the detailed proposals in the Bills. It is important for the comments on individual Bills in this document to be read in conjunction with those consultations and for that purpose the links to the relevant consultations and responses can be found below. These additional consultations may have encouraged people to send responses to the Draft Legislative Programme consultation as well, and vice versa.

Equality Bill

http://www.equalities.gov.uk/publications/Government_Response_to_the_consultation.pdf

http://www.equalities.gov.uk/publications/FRAMEWORK%20FAIRER%20FUTURE.pdf

Organisations that responded to the consultation:
http://www.equalities.gov.uk/equality_bill/a_z-a.htm

Consultation paper http://www.equalities.gov.uk/publications/DLRConsultationbkmk12.pdf

Heritage Protection Bill

http://www.culture.gov.uk/reference_library/publications/5075.aspx

Draft Apprenticeships Bill

The summary of responses to the Public Consultation on the Draft Apprenticeships Bill will be published on the Department for Children, Schools & Families (www.dcsf.gov.uk) and Department for Innovation, Universities & Skills (www.dius.gov.uk) websites in December

Education and Skills Bill

Raising Expectations: Enabling the System to Deliver – Summary of the Events and Written Responses http://www.dfes.gov.uk/consultations/downloadableDocs/RAISING%20EXPECTATIONS%20Summary%20events.pdf

Raising Expectations: Enabling the System to Deliver – Update and next steps http://www.dfes.gov.uk/consultations/downloadableDocs/Microsoft%20Word%20-%20NEXT%20STEPS%20FINAL.pdf

Back on Track – a strategy for modernising alternative provision for young people http://www.dcsf.gov.uk/exclusions/uploads/BACK%20ON%20TRACK%20Next%20Steps%20231008%20final%20(3).pdf

Delivering the Children's Plan – Strengthening Children's Trusts: legislative options http://www.dcsf.gov.uk/consultations/conResults.cfm?consultationId=1568

Statutory Guidance for Children's Trusts on the Duty to Co-operate http://www.dcsf.gov.uk/consultations/conResults.cfm?consultationId=1544

Community Empowerment, Housing and Economic Regeneration Bill

Sub-national Economic Development and Regeneration Consultation http://www.berr.gov.uk/whatwedo/regional/sub-national-review/page40430.html

Draft (Partial) Immigration and Citizenship Bill

http://www.bia.homeoffice.gov.uk/sitecontent/documents/policyandlaw/immigrationandcitizenshipbill/

NHS Reform Bill

Our NHS, Our Future: NHS Next Stage Review (including the final report High Quality Care for All)
http://www.dh.gov.uk/en/Healthcare/OurNHSourfuture/index.htm

The NHS Constitution
http://www.dh.gov.uk/en/Publicationsandstatistics/Publications/PublicationsPolicyAndGuidance/DH_085814

Marine and Coastal Access Bill

Government responses to pre-legislative scrutiny and the public consultation on the Draft Marine Bill:
http://www.official-documents.gov.uk/document/cm74/7422/7422.pdf

ANNEX 1 – Representative list of consultation event attendees.

The following organisations were represented at the consultation events. Because of the nature of some of the events, it was not possible to compile a comprehensive attendees list for all events:

50 50 Vision
Advisory, Conciliation and Arbitration Service
Advice for Life
Acorn
Active Faith Communities
Advantage West Midlands
Age Alliance Wales
Age Concern England
Angelou Centre
Anglia Ruskin University
Arts Council England, Yorkshire
Ashford Borough Council
Asset Skills
Association of North East Councils
Bar Council
Barnardos
Barnfield College
Barnsley Council and South Yorkshire Local Authorities Engagement Partnership
Barrow Council
British Association of Settlements and Social Action Centres
Bedford College
Bedfordshire Local Area Agreement Grouping
Bedfordshire Police
Bernardos
Big Lottery
Birmingham Chamber of Commerce
Black and Ethnic Community Organisations' Network
Black Health Agency
Blakeston School
Black and Minority Ethnic Voluntary and Community Sector Regional Panel
Bolsover District Council
Bolton Council
Bolton News
Boston Borough Council

Bradford Metropolitan District Council
Brewin Dolphin
Bridgend College
British Heart Foundation
British Medical Association
British Waterways
British Telecom
Business in the Community (North East)
Business Link Board
Business Link North East
Butterwick Hospice
Cambridge Ethnic Community Forum
Cambridge Regional College
Cambridgeshire and Peterborough Mental Health Partnership
Cambridgeshire County Council
Cambridgeshire Fire and Rescue Service
Cambridgeshire Local Area Agreement Grouping
Cambridgeshire Police
Cambridgeshire Training and Consultancy
Campaign to Protect Rural England
Canty and Co
Carers Wales
Confederation of British Industry
Chamber of Commerce
Chartered Society of Physiotherapists
Cherwell District Council
Cheshire Police
Chiltern District Council
Chorley Council
Churches' Regional Commission in the North East
Citizens Advice Bureaux
Citizenship Foundation Youth Act
City & Guilds Cambridgeshire Chambers of Commerce
Cleveland Army Cadets
Cleveland Camera Enforcement Unit
Communities and Organisations: Growth and Support
Community Matters
Community Network
Community Regeneration Manager
Community Relations Council
Community Safety Officers
Community Ventures Ltd
Confederation of British Industry, North East
Confederation of British Industry, West Midlands and Oxfordshire
Confederation of British Industry, Northern Ireland
Confederation of Passenger Transport Wales

Confederation of West Midlands Chambers of Commerce
Construction Skills
Consumer Council Wales
Cornwall Police
Corus
Craven District Council
Crawley Borough Council
Cumbria County Council
Cumbria Police
Darlington Borough Council
Darlington College
Delphi Automotive Systems
Department of Politics, University of York.
Derby City Council
Derbyshire County Council
Derbyshire Dales District Council
Design Commission Wales
Development Trust Association
Devon Police
Disability North
Dorset Age Partnership
Dorset Chamber of Commerce
Dorset County Council, Affordable Housing Task Group
Dorset County Council, Culture Theme Group
Dorset County Council, Safer Communities Group
Dorset County Council, Thriving Communities Theme Group
Dorset Primary Care Trust
Dorset Regeneration Co. (Dsquared)
Dorset Strategy Partnership
Durham County Council
Durham University
Early Years & Childcare Service
East Midlands Business Forum
East Midlands Chambers of Commerce
East Midlands Rural Affairs Forum
East of England Business Group
East of England Development Agency
East of England Faiths Council
East of England Regional Assembly
East Riding of Yorkshire Council
East of England Business Group
East of England Development Agency
East of England Regional Assembly, Business
Electoral Commission
East of England Strategic Health Authority
East Midlands Development Agency

Employment Skills Partnership
Energy Saving Trust advice centre
Engineering Employers Federation
English Heritage
English Partnerships
Environment Agency
Equality and Human Rights Commission
Essex Local Area Agreement Partnership
Essex Police
Evening Chronicle
Evening Gazette
Executive Head Stockton Borough First Federation
Fairbridge Inner City Youth
Federation of Small Businesses
Federation of Small Businesses West Midlands Policy Unit
First Great Western
FoneFonics
Friends of the Earth
Garforth Community College
Gateshead Council
General Medical Council
Greater Manchester Community Safety Partnership Team
Greater Manchester Police
GMB (Britain's General Union)
Greater Manchester Centre for Voluntary Organisation
Gofal Cymru
Great Yarmouth College
Greater Peterborough Partnership
Gresham Community Council
Groundwork Northwest
Guide Neighbourhoods Network
Hall Garth School
Halton Borough Council
Halton Housing Trust
Haringey Youth Council and Youth Advisers
Hartlepool Citizens Advice Bureau
Hastings Borough Council
Higher Education Funding Council for Wales
Heritage Lottery Fund
Hertfordshire County Council
Hertfordshire Local Area Agreement Grouping
High Clarence Primary
Highways Agency
Home-Start Barnet Young Parents Project
Housing Association
Housing Corporation

Housing Hartlepool
HSBC
Hull City Council
Humber Economic Partnership
Huntingdonshire Regional College
Irish Business and Employers Confederation – Confederation of British Industry Joint Business Council
IKEA
Institute of Directors
INTRAN
Jo Hand Recruitment
Job Centre Plus
John Madejski Academy
JUST West Yorkshire
Justice First
Kendrick School
Knowsley Metropolitan Borough Council
Lamb Weston / Meijer (United Kingdom)
Lambeth College
Lambeth Council
Lancashire Constabulary
Lancashire County Council
Lancashire Police
Lantra Sector Skills Council
Law Society
Learning and Skills Council
Leeds Chamber
Leeds City Council
Leeds City Region
Leicester City Council
Leicester County Council
Lesbian & Gay Foundation
Lincolnshire County Council
Liverpool 0-25 Network
Liverpool Black and Racial Minorities Network
Liverpool City Council
Liverpool Community Network
Liverpool Charity and Voluntary Services
Liverpool Daily Echo
Liverpool Disability Network
Liverpool Faith Network
Liverpool Mutual Homes
Liverpool Senior Citizens Forum
Living East Representative, Sport England
London Youth
Learning and Skills Council

Luton Borough Council
Luton Local Area Authority Grouping
Multi Area Agreement Board
Maiden Erlegh
Make Your Mark
Manchester Evening News
Mandale Developments
MENTER (Minority Ethnic Network)
Merseyside Refugee Forum
Methodist Church in Ireland
Metropolitan Police
Michelin Tyre
Microsoft Government Affairs
Mid-Bedfordshire District Council
Middlesbrough Senior Citizens Forum
Midland Counties Cooperative
Migrant Workers North West
Mind Cymru
Minor Weir Willis
Mothers Against Violence
Museums Libraries & Archives Yorkshire
National Association of Schoolmasters Union of Women Teachers
National Institute of Adult Continuing Education
Natural England
Neighbourhood Watch Co-ordinator
New Life Family Centre, Billingham
Newcastle City Council
Newcastle University Representing
National Health Service East of England
National Health Service Trust
Northern Ireland Committee of the Irish Congress of Trade Unions
National Institute of Adult Continuing Education
Nordcat Community Transport Provider
Norfolk County Council
Norfolk Local Area Agreement Grouping
Norfolk Learning Partnership
North Dorset District Council
North East Assembly
North East Chamber of Commerce
North East Equality and Diversity Coalition
North East Lincolnshire Council
North East Regional Alcohol Forum
North East Rural Affairs Forum
North Lincolnshire Council
North Norfolk District Council
North Tyneside Council

North West Business Insider
North West Equality and Diversity Group
North West Youth Parliament
North Yorkshire County Council
Northamptonshire Action with Communities in Rural England
Northamptonshire County Council
Northern Advisory Group on Disability
Northern Business Forum
Northern Defence Industries
Northern Housing Consortium
Northern Ireland Council for Voluntary Action
Northern Ireland Local Government Association
Northern Ireland Public Service Alliance
Northumberland County Council
Northumberland Fire and Rescue Service
Northumbria University
Northumbrian Water
Norwich and Norfolk Racial Equality Council
Nottingham City Council
Nottingham County Council
North Tyneside Primary Care Trust
North West District Assembly
North West Regional Assembly
Office of Older Person's Commissioner
One North East
One North West
One Voice Network
Opportunity Peterborough
Pendle County Council
Pertemps
Peterborough Adult Learning Service
Peterborough City Council
Peterborough Local Area Agreement Grouping
Peterborough Primary Care Trust
Peterborough Regional College
Police Service of Northern Ireland
Positif Politics
Presbyterian Church
Preston Council
Price Waterhouse Cooper
Probation Service
Property and Performance Cambridgeshire County Council
Reading Borough Council (youth workers)
Reading Girls School
Reading School
Reading University

Redcar and Cleveland Borough Council
Redcar Life
Redcar Neighbourhood Office
Redhouse School
Renew (formerly Renew Tees Valley)
River City Church
Riverside
Rochdale Metropolitan Borough Council
Royal National Institute for the Blind
Royds Community Association (Bradford)
Rutland County Council
Rydale District Council
Ryeish Green School
Salford City Council
Salford City Council
Salix Homes
Screen Yorkshire
Sustainable Development Round Table
Seamer and Hilton Windfarm Action Group
Sefton Council for Voluntary Service
Simon Community
Skelton Junior Football Club
Skills for Care
Social Business Company
South Devon College
South Lakeland District Council
South Oxfordshire District Council
South Tyneside Council
South Workington Partnership
Southend Borough Council
Southend Local Area Agreement Grouping
Southwell Business Park
Sport England Yorkshire
Sports Academy Manager
Sporttrain Wales
St Michael's Fellowship Young Parents Project
Stockton Council
Stockton on Tees Borough Council
Stockton Parent Support
Stoke on Trent Sentinel
Strata Matrix
Streets Ahead
Stretford High School
Stroke Association
Suffolk Coastal District Council
Suffolk County Council

Suffolk Local Area Agreement Grouping
Suffolk Police
Sunderland City Council
Sunderland University Representing
Surrey Heath Borough Council
Tees Valley Joint Strategy Unit
Tees Valley Living
Tees Valley Sport
Teesside University
Teignbridge District Council
Teignbridge Rangers
Thames Gateway South Essex Partnership
The Broads Authority
The East of England Faiths Agency Community Interest Company
The Shropshire Group
The Woodland Trust
Three Rivers Partnership
Thurrock Adult Community College
Thurrock Local Area Authority Grouping
Time Out of The Box
Tower Hamlets Summer University
Travel Watch East Midlands
Tribal in Education
Trades Union Congress North East
Trades Union Congress North West
Trades Union Congress Yorkshire and the Humber
United Kingdom Youth Parliament
Ultimate Homes and Finance
Universities for the North East
University College Newport
University of Cambridge English for Speakers of Other Languages Examinations
University of Teesside
University of Teesside Student Union
University of Wales Institute, Cardiff
Voluntary Arts England
Voluntary Organisations' Network North East
Voluntary Sector North West
VOX Community Empowerment Network
Wakefield Council
Wakefield Metropolitan District Council
Ward Hadaway
Warrington Crime and Disorder Reduction Partnership
Waveney District Council
West Bromwich Building Society
West Middlesbrough Community Manager

West Midlands Business Council
West Midlands Minority Ethnic Business Forum
West Suffolk College
Westwood & Ravensthorpe Development Trust
White Ribbon Campaign
Winchester City Council
Wirral Council
Wirral Partnership Homes
Workers' Education Association
Writtle College
Youth Hostel Association
York City Council
Yorkshire and Humber Assembly
Yorkshire and the Humber Chambers of Commerce
Yorkshire and the Humber Federation of Small Businesses
Yorkshire and the Humber Regional Energy Forum
Yorkshire and the Humber Regional Forum
Yorkshire and the Humber Rural Affairs Forum
Yorkshire Culture
Yorkshire Forward
Yorkshire Futures
Yorkshire Regional Flood Defence Com
Yorkshire Water

ANNEX 2 – List of postal respondents to the consultation.

The Scottish Inter Faith Council
Association of Chief Police Officers in Scotland
The Law Society of Scotland
Bishops' Conference of Scotland
Lesbian, Gay, Bisexual and Trans Youth Scotland
Association of Chief Police Officers in Wales
East of England Business Group
East of England Development Agency
Intertek
The Cardiomyopathy Association
Marfan Association UK
PHG Foundation
SADS UK
Royal College of Nursing
British Business Improvement Districts (BIDs)
Leeds City Council
Age Concern
Universities UK
Fawcett Society
Scarborough Borough Council
Royal College of Physician and Surgeons of Glasgow
Wakefield Metropolitan District Council
Trinity House Lighthouse Authorities
Equality Network
Rural Affairs Forum
Wildlife and Countryside Link
Skills for Justice
Yorkshire and the Humber Regional Forum
Hull City Council
Help the Aged
Mental Health in England
East Midlands Rural Affairs Forum
Kingston Town Centre Management
Sunderland Council
North East Chamber of Commerce
Association of Personal Injury Lawyers
Gateshead Council

In addition, 21 organisations responded to the consultation through the e-Politix briefing paper, and 44 members of the public responded by post.

Printed in the UK by The Stationery Office Limited
on behalf of the Controller of Her Majesty's Stationery Office
ID5992535 12/08

Printed on Paper containing 75% recycled fibre content minimum.